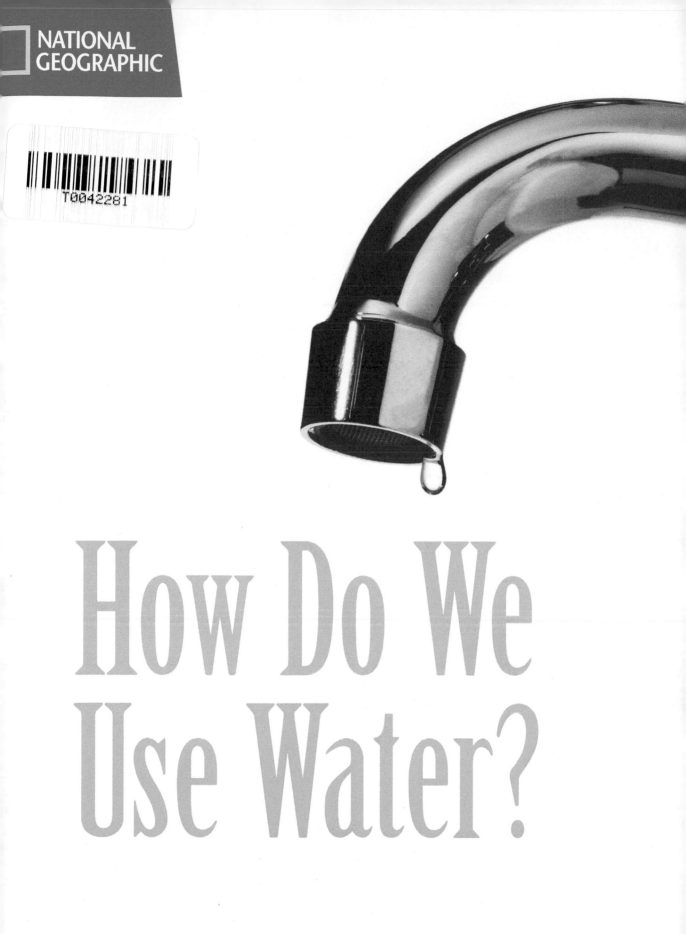

How Do We Use Water?

Beth Geiger

PICTURE CREDITS
Cover, pages 7 (top right), 8-9 (top), 10, 15, 18 (top right), 20, 25 (top left, bottom left, bottom right), 31 (bottom right), 35 (top, second from top), Royalty-Free Corbis; page 1, Brand X Pictures/Getty Images; pages 2-3, Spillway at Chief Joseph Dam on the Columbia River © Paul A.Souder/Corbis; pages 4-5 (top left), 32, 35 (second from bottom), Photodisc Green/Getty Images; pages 4-5 (bottom left), 18-23 (background), 31 (center right), Photodisc Red/Getty Images; page 5 (top right), Photodisc Blue/Getty Images; pages 5 (bottom right), 25 (top right), FoodPix/Getty Images; pages 7 (bottom right), 34 (second from bottom), Robert Harding World Imagery/Getty Images; pages 6-7 (background), 12 (bottom), 36, Masterfile (Royalty-Free Div.) www.masterfile.com; page 8 (top left), Stockbyte/ PictureQuest; page 8 (bottom left), 23, 34 (top), Stone/Getty Images; page 9 (bottom right), Thinkstock/Getty Images; pages 11, 28, The Image Bank/Getty Images; pages 12-13 (top left), Daniel Mirer/Corbis; pages 14, 30 (bottom), 34 (bottom), Caroline Penn/Corbis; pages 16-17, Lonely Planet Images/Getty Images; page 18 (bottom), Panoramic Stock Images/National Geographic Image Collection; page 19, David Mendelsohn/Masterfile www.masterfile.com; pages 21, 35 (bottom), Warren Morgan/Corbis; page 22, John Zoiner/Corbis; page 26 (bottom), George F. Mobley/ National Geographic Image Collection; page 26 (top right), Philip James Corwin/ Corbis; page 27, Gideon Mendel/Corbis; page 29, Anthony Cooper;Ecoscene/ Corbis; page 30 (top), Bruce Peebles/Corbis; page 31 (top left), Digital Vision/Getty Images; page 31 (top right), FK PHOTO/Corbis; page 31 (center left), Creatas/ PictureQuest; page 31 (bottom left), Rob Howard/Corbis; page 34 (second from top), Maria Stenzel/National Geographic Image Collection.

Produced through the worldwide resources of the National Geographic Society, John M. Fahey, Jr., President and Chief Executive Officer; Gilbert M. Grosvenor, Chairman of the Board; Nina D. Hoffman, Executive Vice President and President, Books and Education Publishing Group.

PREPARED BY NATIONAL GEOGRAPHIC SCHOOL PUBLISHING
Ericka Markman, Senior Vice President and President, Children's Books and Education Publishing Group; Steve Mico, Senior Vice President, Editorial Director, Publisher; Francis Downey, Executive Editor; Richard Easby, Editorial Manager; Bea Jackson, Director of Layout and Design; Jim Hiscott, Design Manager; Cynthia Olson, Art Director; Margaret Sidlosky, Illustrations Director; Matt Wascavage, Manager of Publishing Services; Sean Philpotts, Jane Ponton, Production Managers; Ted Tucker, Production Specialist.

MANUFACTURING AND QUALITY CONTROL
Christopher A. Liedel, Chief Financial Officer; Phillip L. Schlosser, Director; Clifton M. Brown III, Manager

CONSULTANT AND REVIEWER
Priti P. Brahma, Ph.D., NOAA/NWS, Silver Spring, Maryland

BOOK DEVELOPMENT
Amy Sarver

◄ People use water to make electricity at this dam in Washington State.

Contents

BOOK DESIGN/PHOTO RESEARCH
3R1 Group, Inc.

Copyright © 2006 National Geographic Society.
All Rights Reserved. Reproduction of the whole or any part of the
contents without written permission from the publisher is prohibited.
National Geographic, National Geographic School Publishing,
National Geographic Reading Expeditions, and the Yellow Border
are registered trademarks of the National Geographic Society.

Published by the National Geographic Society
1145 17th Street N.W.
Washington, D.C. 20036-4688

ISBN-13: 978-07922-5429-4
ISBN-10: 07922-5429-5

2010 2009 2008 2007 2006
   5 6 7 8 9 10 21 20 19 18

Printed in the United States of America

▲ People use water to wash their hands.

Using Water

Every day, you use water. You use it for washing your hands. You use water for brushing your teeth. You also drink water. You might be surprised by how much water you use each day.

Look at the pictures.

- What does each picture show?
- How do people use water?
- Why is water important?

▲ People use water to help plants grow.

▲ People use water to wash
their cars.

▲ People
drink water.

Big Idea

People use water in many ways.

Set Purpose

Learn about ways that people use water.

Questions You Will Explore

Where do we get fresh water?

How do we use fresh water?

How Do People Use Water?

There is a lot of water on Earth. But most of the water is in the ocean. Ocean water is **salt water**. People cannot drink salt water.

We can drink only **fresh water**. There is much less fresh water on Earth than salt water. But fresh water is much more useful to people. Most of the water we use is fresh water.

....

salt water – water that contains a large amount of salt

fresh water – water that does not have large amounts of salt

Salt Water

Water in the ocean is salt water.

Fresh Water

Water in rivers, lakes, and streams is fresh water.

DRINKING WATER | People drink fresh water.

LOSING WATER | People lose water when they sweat.

Drinking Water

You need to drink water to live. Why? Most of your body is made of water. Your blood is mostly water. Water keeps your heart and brain working properly. Water is an important part of you.

All day, you lose water from your body. You lose it when you sweat. You also lose water when you get rid of waste. That is why you need to drink plenty of water each day. You need to replace the water you lose.

▲ People use fresh water to wash dishes.

Water for Everyday Living

You use water in other ways, too. You use water to do many activities each day. Just think about the water you use to wash dishes and cook. You use water to brush your teeth. You also use a lot of water when you take a shower or bath.

▶ You use water to brush your teeth.

WATER FOR FARMING | Farmers use fresh water to irrigate their crops.

Water for Farming

Farmers use a lot of fresh water. They use water to grow **crops**. Crops are plants that people grow to sell. Much of the fresh water in the United States is used for farming.

Many farms are in areas without much rainfall. Farmers **irrigate** to keep their crops alive. This means the farmers use water other than rain to water their crops.

crop – a kind of plant that people grow to sell

irrigate – to supply land with water other than rain

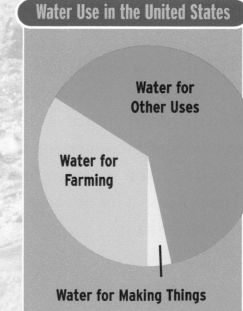

Water Use in the United States

Water for Other Uses

Water for Farming

Water for Making Things

WATER FOR MAKING THINGS People use water when they make concrete.

Water for Making Things

People also use water to make things. Just think about building a house. Water is used to mix concrete. Concrete can be used to make floors and walls. Water is also used to make paint. People use paint to add color to their homes.

Water is also used to make metal and glass. It would be hard to build a house without these materials. All these materials are made with the help of water.

Some water parks use thousands of gallons of water each day.

Water Play

People use water for fun. Everyone loves to play in water on a hot day. Swimming pools and water parks are great places to cool down.

But having fun uses up a lot of water. Just think about a water park. They have pools, waterslides, and wave machines. These use millions of gallons of water.

► People use water to have fun when it is hot outside.

The water a person uses each day would fill two and a half bathtubs.

It All Adds Up!

People depend on fresh water every day. They use it for drinking, for making things, and for fun. People in the United States use a lot of water. Each person uses about 378 liters (100 gallons) of water each day. That amount of water would fill two and a half bathtubs. That is a lot of water!

▼ Some people use pumps to pull fresh water out of the ground.

Where We Find Fresh Water

Where does all the fresh water come from? People get most of the fresh water they need from Earth's surface. This is called **surface water.** It comes mainly from rivers and lakes. People also use **groundwater.** This is water found in the ground. Pumps are used to pull this water to the surface.

surface water – fresh water found on Earth's surface, such as in rivers or lakes

groundwater – water found in the ground

Fresh Water on Earth

Frozen water

Groundwater

Lakes, rivers, and water in air

▲ Most of Earth's fresh water
is frozen.

Frozen Fresh Water

Fresh water is found in many places. But most of Earth's fresh water is frozen. In some places, the land is covered with frozen water. Yet people cannot easily use fresh water that is frozen.

So people get their fresh water from rivers and lakes. They also pump fresh water from the ground. These sources make up a very small part of the fresh water on Earth. Yet each day, people use this water in many ways.

Stop and Think!

How do people use fresh water?

Water

Recap
Explain how people
use water.

Set Purpose
Learn how people
use water from the
Columbia River.

at Work

The Columbia River is an important river. It flows through the states of Oregon and Washington. Then it empties into the Pacific Ocean. Millions of people depend on the water in the Columbia River. How do they use it?

Columbia River

Growing Cherries

It is 5 a.m. and it is still dark outside. But Kevin Aiken has been awake for an hour. Kevin is a farmer. He grows cherries near Wenatchee, Washington. How does Kevin make sure the cherries get enough water? He stops at an irrigation pipe. He turns a big wheel on the pipe. Water begins to spout from dozens of sprinklers under the cherry trees.

This area does not get enough rain to grow fruit trees. So Kevin uses water from the Columbia River to water the trees. Pumps move the river water to the cherry trees.

▼ Water from the Columbia is used to grow cherry trees.

Water to Drink

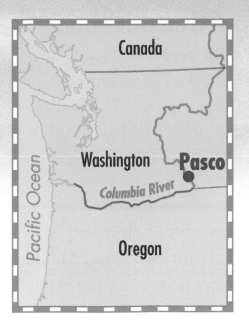

Farther down the Columbia River is the city of Pasco. Pasco is also in Washington State. In Pasco, Roberto Lopez plays basketball at his school. Roberto stops for a drink of water after playing. The water Roberto drinks comes from the Columbia River.

Before the water gets to Roberto's school, it has to be cleaned. The water is cleaned in a water treatment plant. People cannot safely drink water right out of rivers. It always needs to be cleaned first.

▼ **Water is cleaned in a water treatment plant.**

Water Power

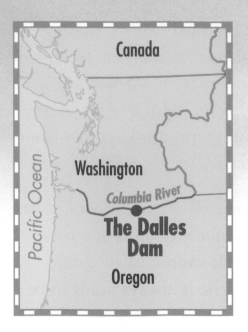

Farther down the river is the Dalles Dam. A dam is a barrier built across a river. A dam holds the water back. The water can then be used for different things. The Dalles Dam makes electricity. Water rushes through the dam. The water turns machines that make electricity.

The Dalles Dam makes a lot of electricity. It makes enough electricity for two cities. Making electricity is another way people use the water from the Columbia River.

▼ The Dalles Dam makes electricity.

Water Fun

Downstream, Shana Sweitzer wakes up early. Shana is a **windsurfer**. She lives in a city called Hood River. It is in Oregon State beside the Columbia River. Shana grabs a bite to eat. Then she rushes to the river. She jumps on her windsurfing board. She sails across the river. Like Shana, many people use the river for fun.

windsurfer – a person who rides over water on a board with a sail

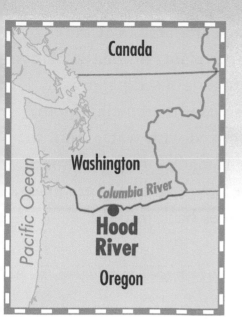

▼ **A windsurfer uses the river for fun.**

Canada

Washington
Longview

Pacific Ocean

Columbia River

Oregon

Boxes and Bags

Down the river, the water arrives at the Longview Fibre paper plant. Inside the plant, Alan Whitford watches as used paper is dumped into tanks wider than a classroom. The used paper is mixed with water from the river. This mixture is made into paper boxes and bags. After the boxes and bags are made, most of the water goes back into the Columbia River.

▼ **These big rolls of paper are made in a paper plant.**

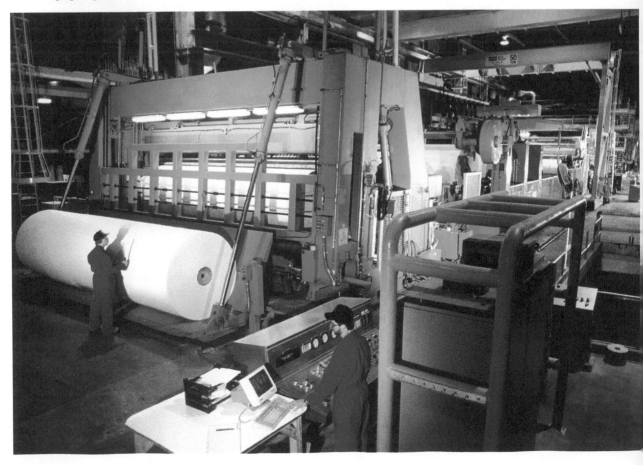

Carrying Goods

Many boats carry things along the Columbia River. One type of boat is called a **barge**. A barge is a long, flat boat. It can carry many kinds of goods. Some barges carry wheat. Others carry fuel. Many kinds of goods travel on the river. The barges take their goods to cities like Astoria. Astoria is located near the Pacific Ocean.

barge – a long, flat boat that carries goods

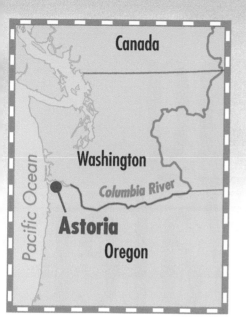

▼ **This barge moves goods.**

Stop and Think!

HOW do people use water from the Columbia River?

23

Recap
Tell how people use the water in the Columbia River.

Set Purpose
Read these articles to learn more about how people use water.

Using Water

Most of Earth's water is salt water. Yet most of the water that people use is fresh water.

Here are some ideas you learned about fresh water.

- Most of the water people use each day is fresh water.
- People use fresh water for drinking and cleaning.
- People use fresh water for farming and for making things.
- Most of Earth's fresh water is frozen.

Check What You Have Learned

What do the photos show about fresh water?

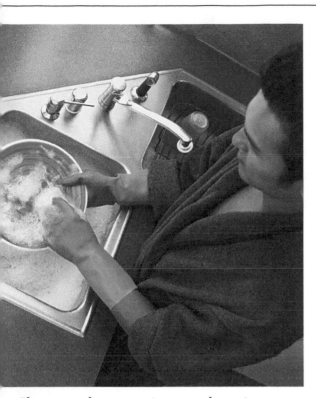

▲ The water that comes into your home is fresh water.

▲ People drink fresh water.

▲ Farmers use water to irrigate their crops.

▲ Most of the fresh water on Earth is frozen.

Sharing the Columbia

People are not the only living things that use the Columbia River. For thousands of years, salmon have traveled along it. Today, there are dams along the river. The dams can block the flow of river water. How do the salmon travel up the river? People have built fish ladders beside the dams. These are steps with water flowing over them. The fish ladders let the salmon travel along the river, even where there are dams.

▼ Salmon can get around dams by swimming up fish ladders.

▼ A fish ladder has steps that let salmon move around a river dam.

World Water Use

An American uses about 378 liters (100 gallons) of water per day. But people in some places get by on less. In Europe, the average person uses just 200 liters (53 gallons) per day. In dry regions of Africa, a person may use just 11 to 18 liters (3 to 5 gallons) per day!

▶ **People in other parts of the world use less water than Americans.**

Native Plants

Why do people not water trees in the wilderness? That is because the trees are a type of native plant. That means they are plants that have lived in a certain area for many years. Native plants are used to the rainfall in a certain area. So they do not need extra watering.

▼ These native plants in Utah do not need extra watering.

◀ Some people use barrels to collect rainwater from their roofs.

Reusing Rain

Rain is a great source of fresh water. Why not collect it? Some people do. People collect rain from the roofs of their homes. The rain runs down the roofs and into barrels. Then, people can use the rainwater to water their gardens.

A lot of rain can fall on a roof. Some people collect as much as 1,514 liters (400 gallons) from one big rainstorm.

Many kinds of words are used in this book. Here you will learn about compound words. You will also learn about multiple-meaning words.

Compound Words

Compound words are made by joining two shorter words. Find the compound words below. What smaller words form each compound word?

rain + fall = rainfall

The **rainfall** lasted an hour.

ground + water = groundwater

People pump **groundwater.**

Multiple-Meaning Words

Multiple-meaning words are words with more than one meaning. What two meanings do each of these words have?

Drops of water fall from the faucet.

She **drops** her change into her purse.

She uses water to **brush** her teeth.

She uses the **brush** to paint.

The lake is full of **water.**

The irrigation sprinklers **water** the plants.

Write About Water Use

How much water do you use? Research to find out. Keep a water journal to record how much water you use.

Research

List all of the ways that you use water in one day.

Take Notes

Take notes to tell how much water you used with each activity. For example, if you took a shower, write down how long the water was running.

Write

At the end of the day, make a chart showing the ways that you used water. Write a paragraph that tells what activities used the most water.

Read and Compare

Read More About Water

Find and read other books about water. As you read, think about these questions.

- How do people use water?
- Why is water important?
- How do scientists learn about water on Earth?

Books to Read

▲ Read about water and its properties.

▲ Read about the water in Earth's oceans.

▲ Read about water in the sky and on Earth's surface.

Glossary

barge (page 23)
A long, flat boat that carries goods
The barge carries goods along the Columbia River.

crop (page 10)
A kind of plant that people grow to sell
Corn is a crop that farmers grow and sell.

KEY CONCEPT

fresh water (page 7)
Water that does not have large amounts of salt
Most of Earth's fresh water is frozen.

KEY CONCEPT

groundwater (page 14)
Water found in the ground
People pump groundwater.

irrigate (page 10)
To supply land with water other than rain
The farmers irrigate their crops.

salt water (page 7)
Water that contains a large amount of salt
Oceans are made of salt water.

surface water (page 14)
Fresh water found on Earth's surface, such as in
rivers or lakes
The surface water in most lakes is fresh water.

windsurfer (page 21)
A person who rides over water on a board with a sail
The windsurfer moves across the water.

Index